Forgiving
MADNESS

Forgiving MADNESS

POETRY AND PROSE
BY

A.M. FORNEY

300 SOUTH MEDIA GROUP
NEW YORK

FORGIVING MADNESS

ISBN-13: 978-1-957596-19-8 (paperback)
ISBN-13: 978-1-957596-20-4 (ebook)

Cover & Interior Design by Indie Author Solutions
Published by 300 South Media Group

To Roman, Avana and Titan.
Too much peacocks!

TABLE OF CONTENTS

VOMIT OF THE BRAIN

DEAR DIARY

FATHER MISERY

UNIMPRESSED IMPRESSION

DIAGNOSIS

SOBER

THE DRIVE

WINTER

A PLETHORA OF RANDOMNESS

WORDS WITHIN THE DARKNESS

VOMIT OF THE BRAIN

It won't shut off
It won't be tame
I am able to write
Because I suffer from vomit of the brain
Memories or thoughts, never let up
Sit down with one, soon pour a second cup
I write and I write
Until my fingers are numb
At first, I did worry
Readers would think it was dumb
To pour out my words
My thoughts and my pain
But it's something I can't help
Because I have vomit of the brain

Dear Diary

SICK MAN'S SLAVE

When children are little
They're meant to be innocent
Not taken and forced to
Be a sick man's slave

I'M FREE

The wind chills my spine
Black coffee will be fine
Facing monsters today
Demons to slay
Tough woman, I must be
From his hold, I am free

THE SCENT OF VANILLA

the scent of vanilla makes her skin crawl
bad memories, now a waterfall
she hides her emotions, ignores the scars
she only finds comfort, in looking at the stars
it's not just vanilla
it's other things too
that make her remember
what pedophiles do

STUNTED

Is a rose still a rose
If a storm stunted it's thorns
And the part never grows

ROT

It burns deep down
When memories replay
You remind yourself
It's the past and you're okay
But you can't help the flashbacks
They seem to trickle in
Convincing you that you are
Broken within
Broken is what you definitely are not
Forget about the past
And wish for him to rot

SUFFERING

I said I'd forgive him
I do and I will
But knowing he is suffering
Will always give me a thrill
I knew no better, just a child
Manipulated and twisted, a broken little girl

SINKING BOAT

if you know and you ignore
if you know and you cover
you're sick
you're twisted
the boat will sink soon enough

RUINED

Would someone care so much
if they knew the you that we knew
They ruined a young girl
and destroyed her before she grew

REPULSIVE MEMORIES

press erase in your brain
and then, you will find
you're way better off
with the repulsive memories behind

PRAYING FOR YOUR FALL

while you may think you won
you've lost so much of it all
now, I'll sit back
and pray for your fall

FIGHTER

to have childhood trauma
it alters some things
the way your brain processes
what emotions you bring
when sitting alone
or in a group of more
sometimes, simply getting out of bed
feels like a chore
but at one point or another, we learn to let go
you're allowed to still mourn, rightfully so
but honey, close the book
put it up on the shelf
adopt a new outlook
you can help heal yourself
it's never too late
you're not broken
you're cracked
you've grown into yourself
you've learned a lot that you lacked
this new, happy person will feel a lot lighter
after all you've been through
you deserve it, because you're a fighter

HEALING

Her veins
Flowing with pain
The memories and flashbacks
Replay in her brain
She talks herself down
Get off that ledge
Healing herself
Has become her only pledge

Father
Misery

AUTOMATIC DEFENSE

You don't just wake up this way
Things build and build
Causing you to mold into something
you have to be
as an automatic defense

DOLLS

they don't belong to you
you know that they don't
but keeping them is your nature
because giving back, you won't

MISERY PRONE

We come into the world because of two people
So how is it to feel when you're left stranded by one
Standing alone
Figuring life out, basically on your own
Sad
Depressed
Resentful
Mad
There is good to this, though
A silver lining, if you will
To have the satisfaction of knowing
   you're allowed to feel how you feel
Your thoughts are valid
   and your conscience can be clear
You need to know,
   they're not the only reason you're here
You will never be the father you have been given,
   simply a blood relative of
You will grow to be better than he is,
you will learn to properly love
Don't burden yourself with the questions,
   why this or why that
The truth is, it doesn't matter
You owe him nothing
The earlier life and "I love you"s
Were simply, him bluffing
Hold your head high, love the ones who stay
Close your eyes
Let it go
Let it float away
With this new peace, you will find
You're not so alone
For, he is the one who is misery prone

HE WILL BE LONELY

You shut me out and locked the door
I've thought about it more and more
Why do I bother, you may ask
Because in therapy, it's become a task
To talk of the hurt that you caused me
And to realize how lonely you'll always be

MAGNETIC

Magnetic pain
Grips at her thoughts
Magnetic failure
Tickles her heart
Magnetic forgiveness
Escapes her soul

Unimpressed Impression

TRENDY

please don't keep doing things
just because they're trendy and cool
to those of us watching
you just look like a fool

HUMAN MOSQUITOES

People will always come in and out of your life
Be cautious of those who only stay when there's strife
They're human mosquitoes
Your blood is their fuel
They live for the drama that occasionally comes
When there is no chaos to be had
you're left, twiddling your thumbs
it may take a day, a month or several years
but when you see a glimpse of their fangs
Trust and believe, it is how it appears

PROBABLY YOU

There are a handful of people
I will never admit that I knew
If you're questioning who
Then, it's probably you too

JUDGEMENT

Do not judge those who have judged you
for then, you're at the same level
and that simply is not true

GOODBYE

She's the type of girl that will stay by your side
Being honest and truthful, you'll never ask if she's lied
But while she will continuously take being ignored and
neglected
Don't bother to ask why when it's goodbye, she's
selected

GAME OVER

she has no time or patience
she shouldn't have from the start
the only reason she did
was because she's been cursed with a big heart
you sit and you judge, talk and take aim
but what happens when she's caught on
and no longer plays your little game

LET DOWN

Everyone has done it
It is nothing new
But there is now a brick wall
That no one will get through

EXPECTED AMNESIA

They cut you with words
You always forgive
They expect you to forget
But how can you, and live
Your fullest, happiest, best life
Knowing you're carrying around
Such awful pain and strife
So don't forgive and don't forget
This new found strength will be
The best yet

A GOOD PERSON

A good person is one to not shove
because below the belt is where anger isn't above

SECRETS

The secrets I know
could ruin their life
and rightfully so
but zipped, the lips stay
because that's just not my way

MILKING THE DIME

it's always a laugh to be used by a friend
but how many times until you call it the end
stealing ideas and words right out of your mouth
it was a matter of time before it all went south
so steal any follows and milk others dime
for you, my dear buddy, I no longer have time

WOMAN

and then, she got to a place
where she didn't care if you were the same behind her
back
as you pretend to her face
it's okay, she knows more than you think she does
she's just grown into a better person
but she's not the girl that she was
she prefers to be called "woman" and not have "girl" as
a label
and she wants to see you eat
just not at her table

JEALOUSY

when someone is only happy
when you're depressed or sad
it may be the time to open your eyes
just a tad
now, realizing that jealousy actually played a part
you've forgiven and moved on
they're out of your heart

DISSECTING

she has taken a moment
she's dissecting things in her brain
with all the chaos that's brought to her
it's a shock, she's still sane

STEPPING STONE

you used her as a stepping stone
and that's okay
you avoid her, ignore her
then pretend close, you'll stay
like you're close
still friends
like you didn't burn the candle at both ends
she was all you had
when you had no one else
you should try to remember
because you will end up by yourself
she won't be there
she'll be a memory
upon a dusty shelf

FAKE PAL

I'm paying close attention to who's around now
and who's sending me messages, to be a fake pal
I know who is real
and I know who is not
some of you were trash talking me
and think I forgot
I'll ignore you, delete you and maybe block you too
I know my true friends
and there are very few

DISMISSAL

after weeks of soul searching and questioning things
I'm excited to move forward and see what life brings
If you can't support the things that I've changed
your dismissal from my life can definitely be arranged

BASHING YOU

the only people who will continually bash you
are the ones who know
that they'll never pass you

UNDESERVED RESPECT

I searched and searched
but I couldn't find
a quote that could cover
what I had in mind
to keep criticizing children
makes you sick and disturbed
so don't sit there and wonder
why your respect isn't deserved

EASY TARGET

you're an easy target
the mark always on your back
you're an easy target
not sure why you've never been granted slack
you're an easy target
when silence creeps in, but your mind, it still screams
you're an easy target
you should have known back then
that nothing is what it seems
you're an easy target

YOU'RE NOT EVERYTHING

you're not everything to everyone
you're barely even something
you try and try to be
to even be a small glimmer of matter
you fall and fall
they don't want you to be
you're a glimmer of nothing
all that you are
to them
is nothing

INVISIBLE FAIRNESS

Nothing in her life ever seemed normal
or fair
She couldn't even look back
And the same friends be there
Many of her family
Treated her the same way too
As if she were a shadow
Invisible
Or see thru

BACKBONE

pushed to the ground
constantly put down
forever broken
one day, you wake up
strength in your back
like never before
you've grown a backbone
time to switch up the usual
change up the current
move things along
no longer broken
you've got a backbone

CUP OF TEA

you won't be everyone's cup of tea
oil and water can be family
don't lose your desire, hope or energy
keep pushing forward
and be all that you can be

THE FEELING OF INADEQUACY

the feeling of inadequacy
it lingers within
will she ever be good enough
enough to celebrate her wins

LIES

taking a deep look within
each new path I take
waiting for the judgement to begin
but when I'm happy with who I am
nothing you say
makes me give a damn
I know what I can do
and what I cannot
it seems, the past, you have forgot
I never let my guard down
never let up the ties
knew you'd never support me
knew you'd spread awful lies
it's okay
I'm moving on
that was that
and now, I'm gone

Diagnosis

SHE'S COMPLEX

She's complex
There are levels
And layers to her soul
But when you see inside her
You'll see her heart of gold

NOTHINGNESS

In the darkness, she finds herself
for that is where nothingness resides
it's all right there
yet there, it also hides

BRICKS

she's different
at least, that's what they say
she's on cloud nine
bawling, the next day
showing a huge smile
making everyone around her laugh
feeling piles of bricks inside
hoping the feeling will soon pass
if complex is what they call it
then, that's what she is
she just knows deep down
she is better than this
better than how she feels
low, down
happy, not allowed
one day, hopefully soon
she will be back on that cloud

REGRESSION

Darkness
Not even the shimmer of a star
Pushing herself
Only to pull back way too far

HUMAN

The tenseness of her body
Is the only feeling that reminds her
She's human

SEPARATED HELL

When you can't help but feel different from everybody
else
There are times when you just sit alone and cry
You don't tell the professionals
but there are times you just hope to die
Your soul and your person don't feel like the same
Like there's two of you and each one has a different
name
A different personality, a different brain
You see monsters and demons,
you thought that they had been slain
but then, there's a time that you snap out of it
Where you feel like the one person for just a little bit
Happier person. The better one.
The one who laughs, jokes and likes to have fun
So which one are you
Are you the soul or the shell
Will you forever be living in this torturous, separated
hell?

PILL

This medicine gives me heartburn in my chest
I decided to start it, to give my mind a rest
From all of the chaos and all of the stress
To help lift me up and be less depressed
Will it work, will it make a difference?
In my brain, I'd just like a moment of silence
Just to relax, just to be chill
That calmness from sitting, looking out from the
windowsill
On a rainy day or a snowy night
I just want to know
It'll all be alright

SHE IS

With a deep breath
She realizes
She is not the trauma
She is not the past
She is the present
She is the future

PICKING AND PULLING

Because you can just feel
When the vibe is off
The stress is there
You're picking and pulling
Your skin and your hair
You know it's off
You don't know how to align
To leave the trauma
All the bad memories
Behind

CHAOTIC MIND

I hate when I'm wide awake and I can't sleep
Late at night
My mind just simply won't turn off
Anxiety, no end in sight
Am I a good enough mother, wife and friend?
I would pay a pretty penny
For all of this worry to end

PAIN BEHIND

She thought things couldn't get better
She thought it was the end
She sat and she questioned
Who was her true friend
After sifting and searching
She truly did find
She was able to move on
And leave the pain all behind

SANITY

Sometimes, digging deep
and tapping into memories
bad or good
is the best thing for our sanity

DIAGNOSIS

Is it truly depression, bipolar and PTSD
she wants someone to find out
she wants someone to finally see

BIPOLAR BRAIN

Her moods change with the seasons
like soft, untouched snow
everything she knew
she wants to learn to un-know

TWO PEOPLE

She always felt like two people
sometimes three
sometimes four
trying to recover
she closed a different door
on one person
two
three
four
but then, she discovered
there had already been more
just beneath the surface
right under her skin
the angels and demons
forever fighting to win
the dark thoughts and memories
forever, they'll stay
and all the people she is
are never going away

SHE IS WHO SHE IS

She is who she is
no doubts and no lies
she is who she is
even though she hides
she is who she is
that's her, looking inside
she is who she is
and the rules, she'll abide

DISRUPTIVE BEAUTY

she is like the ocean
calm with waves of disruption
either way, beautiful

LINGERING DEMONS

who are you, really?
you don't even know
who are you trying
so desperately
to let go
the demons of the past will always linger
don't call names
don't judge
and don't point your finger
you may be better now
but you weren't back then
you wouldn't have even wanted
to be your own friend

FAMILIAR SCARS

Familiar scars
Begin to show
From a time when she
Was oh, so low
On her body
They're like unique art
From the beginning, she wishes
She could restart
But the scars go deeper
They sink further in
All the trauma is buried
Deep, deep within

STIGMA

a headache
you poor thing
a cold
get some rest
a toothache
that has to hurt
depressed and cannot function
shake it off
they claim it's a silly spurt

UNINFORMED HYPOCRISY

there are so many things that she does not share
for fear of judgement
lack of care
a society full of uninformed hypocrisy
a brave face and pretty smile, is all you will see
over a decade of being told that she was one way
to find out it was all wrong, does not feel okay
but the shock has worn off
and the tears have stopped their flow
now, she knows she has to be herself
that's the only person to show

TRIGGER

you're okay for a day, weeks, maybe a month
then the littlest thing makes you change at once
insecurities are loud and easy to find
you thought you repaired it
and left it behind
to cut it open and see inside
see everything you desperately hide

BARBED WIRE ROPE

the end of her rope feels like a barbed wire fence
her head is spinning, depression intense
her emotions cannot stay in place
she feels like with no shoes, she's running a race
each step cuts and burns
for her life to be normal, she desperately yearns
her heart hurts like someone has a grip and won't let go
can it just be Monday, so then, she will know
does she deserve her life back
deserve a second chance
can it just be water under the bridge
at that water, she will never even glance

IT WAS HER

it was her
she went through it all
because of her
always carrying the blame
it just isn't the same
it wasn't she, little girl
it was her

WHIRLWIND OF MADNESS

it's a whirlwind
going a million miles a minute
spins and spins
your mind is a volcano
of all kinds of thoughts
memories and fears
paranoia for now and over years
you can't control the eruption
you try
frustration weighs in
what are these feelings
when did they begin
it was sometime tonight
earlier in the day
you felt them creep up
but you kept them at bay
but not, it's erupting
the volcanic ash flows down
you smile but you're still wearing a frown
why is this happening
why right this second
can you just forget it
recall good thoughts to reckon
you'll try to sleep
try to forget all this sadness
you'll try to sleep
and turn your brain off of the madness

DIM

the path was dark
and then, it was dim
she had to find
the light within
to light the path
to find her way
and now, she knows
she'll be okay

ACIDIC RAIN

black swirls into total darkness
the ride has just begun
this is her life
her illness
it seems to never end
the adrenaline kicking in
sadness rains upon her like acid
she hurts
but she can't escape

THE SAME NEW

it's not hard to find yourself
will you like what you find
the person you thought you've been
is someone you want to leave behind
you'll notice the people who fall away
because their negativity
just cannot stay
it's an automatic response
something beyond control
only gravitating toward positive
like a magnetic pull
so let go of who you have always been
let this be the start
just be the new you
the you
you've always been in your heart

SHE KNEW

at the core, she knew
she could just feel
who destiny meant for her to be
positive
light
any wrongs
made right
she knew
change ahead
fear behind
clearing her heart
cleansing her mind
she knew

MASK

You wake from a dream
You feel as if it were real
Knowing now
How your subconscious truly feels
You discover, you're holding onto
something
You can't see it clear
But deep within you, you start to feel fear
What if it was real?
The dream wasn't subconscious thoughts
But twisted ideas your mind has yet to plot
Against you
Against those you love
What are you holding, you just want to see
A mirror, you find
Reflection, so clear
It's so pretty
So lifelike and believable
But it isn't, it's dark, dark and evil
What you're holding, show it to us all
A mask
It's a mask, you turn and it falls

ZIPPERS

Why doesn't our skin have zippers?
When we feel like we are trapped inside
Our only option is to attempt to hide
But it's like a monster that dwells
The nerves and mind swell
With worry and self doubt
Your mind, you could live without
But if we just came with zippers
Life would be simpler
Take off the layer
Show who you feel like today
Tomorrow, it's another role you'll play

CAVING IN

is it possible to feel
like your insides are caving in
you try and push through
but it seems, you never win
you're almost ahead
you almost see the light
you've tripped and you've fallen
now, it's nowhere in sight

YOU'RE ALRIGHT

I don't think we get over things
I think we push them back
We think of only good times
We ignore all of the black
Hurt as a child can never be touched
It's your own hand
You need to learn to clutch
Because the ones you needed the most
Didn't need you as much
We don't forget the bad times
They will come to light
And it's okay to know
That for now
You're alright

Sober

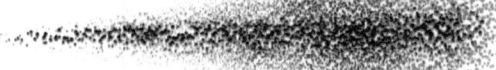

THE DEVIL IN THE BOTTLE

Some say alcohol is the devil
and she's finding that is true
for, it seems that it's the answer
of why'd you do that thing you do

QUITTERS STRENGTH

Saying "I don't drink" is okay
It's not a chore
But it is hard to give up something
That is everywhere, galore

NEW YEAR

A new year is a good time to reflect
but use the time not to waste on regret
Use it on hope for the fresh path ahead

HEALING FEELING

just because you've put a stop to it
doesn't mean you won't feel
allow yourself that
just remember to heal

BOTTLE MIRROR

I can't do it alone
for years and years, I've tried
each time I've tried to quit
it just seems that I've lied
but something has changed
and I'm realizing my goals
and anyone who doubts me
I'll prove them all fools

CHANGE

when you want it to change
but you're just not sure how
you keep putting it off
but it's what you need now
it's normal, relaxing and usually fun
but deep, deep down
you know you have to be done

DO NOT TURN BACK

it's okay to fall off
as long as you start again
and do not turn back
to where it began

PEACEFUL HAPPINESS

And she was happy
She was at peace
She let go
And felt a new kind of release

WALLS OF IRON

The walls of iron
made of pure steel
slowly fell down
as I desired to feel

LAST TIME

I've heard it said before
but I didn't know it was true
there will always be a last time
that you do a thing you do

BE BETTER

the choice to better oneself
does not come from that person feeling inadequate
it comes from a place of imbalance
a place, which when reflected upon
makes the mirror and brain fog up and crack
the want to better oneself
is wanting just that
one wanting to be better
not because of anything they lack

Spiritual Journey

EMPATHETIC SOUL

she can feel their energy
sense their pain
sometimes, it feels like
she is going insane

PLUVIOPHILE

she used to hate the rain
until she realized
the feeling it brings
never truly leaves

IN THE NIGHT

The truth is in the night
When the sky is dark
The lights are dim
Relax and let
The calmness of the moon in

GIFTS OF EARTH

The earth has so many gifts
if you open your eyes
the tiniest of things
catches you by surprise

SUBCONSCIOUS MIND

it's a spiritual journey
you've tried it before
but, you gave up on trying
and searching for more
you want to discover
you want to find
and try to tap into
your subconscious mind

HUMAN ILLUSION

Life is an illusion
nothing is truly real
but that doesn't make it true
that you can't feel how you feel
we are simply just humans
going through this experience
but again, we will be back to have
another life since

A PLANET FOR ONE

into another galaxy
a planet for one
washing away
all of the bad that's been done
new exploration
this different place
a multitude of memories
you came here to erase

Short &
Penned

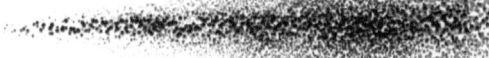

THE RAIN OF CHANGE

The rain of change
Waters the seeds
That bloom into the best life

AMETHYST

She daydreams of a small gold ring
center of amethyst
she feels her heart sing

SOUL RIVER

the embers of her soul
are landing on the river of her past

HER AURA

Her aura?
The smoke of a smoldering flame that is her past

SPARKLES

Her soul sparkles with the embers of perseverance and strength

OPPOSITION

When the mirror reflects the soul of opposition

MIDDLE GROUND

She's somewhere between strong and broken

OCEAN

The words flooded her brain like the waves of an ocean
Crashing against the sand and back again

THE DESIRE

The desire to be whole
Is not the result of being broken

LOUD

The mind screams in silence

HOPE

Her veins glisten with hope

MATCH OF LIFE

Light the soul
with the match of life

FOLDED

When the sea of sequins folded to a lake of darkness

THOUGHTS

Her thoughts are as deep as the ocean

RESPONSE

Power is silence
Silence is power

MAGNET FOR THE COLD

Having a heart of gold
Is like a magnet for the cold

LOST

The best part to lose
is the part without benefit

THE CALM

The calm is worth the storm

CRASH

The ocean of happiness crashes
into the lake of nothingness

REFLECTIVE SOUL

Her writings are dark
For, that is what her soul reflects

REFLECTION

Shallow water still reflects

LET GO

Strong people forgive
Unbreakable people let go

SHORT FAIRYTALE

Once upon a time
She forgot who she was
Once upon a time

ENOUGH

The echoes from her screams
told her she was enough

HER SOUL

In the blizzard that is life
she found her soul

POWERFUL INTUITION

The powerful feeling when the soul is guided
by sheer heartfelt intuition

BECOMING YOU

Looking within takes strength
Becoming who you find
takes courage

BED

it is a portal to a timed paradise
-bed

BLURRED BEAUTY

Sand is beautiful
but when it's made up of who you use to be
it's hard to see beauty

BLEEDING

Her soul bleeds to see
And get to know
The part of her
That she tried to let go

TEARS

She can't see herself through the foggy tears

TWIST

in a weird twist of pain
the feather tickles her veins

FROZEN IN REWIND

today's a big day
and nobody knows it
it feels like the past
if we rewound and froze it

BROKEN BEAUTY

Even the beautiful keys of a piano can break

OCEAN MIND

her thoughts flow with the wind
her mind, an ocean

ACHING SOUL

her soul ached to hear
the words that were oozing from her skin

VIBES

vibes don't lie
you know what you feel
vibes don't lie
weed out who isn't real

BLOOMED DEATH

When you're gifted flowers
Do you remember all the ones of the past
that have died and never bloomed again?

UMBRELLA

the rain is not letting up
it won't
it can't

EMPTINESS

There comes a time when
content and comfortable turns
into exhaustion and emptiness

WEAK

Her typical poems
address "her" and "she"
because to say "I"
would make her feel weak

FLOAT ON

We all float to
and drift toward
the path we belong on

The
Drive

MOTIVATION

go for your goals
make sure you see them through
because you've got to know
you can only depend on you

GREAT

She didn't know what was ahead
the path before her, paved by fate
She didn't know what to do or be
but whatever it was, she was determined to be great

TO THE START

Lead me into the darkness
I want a better reputation
Take me to the start
Help me exceed their expectations

DIG DEEPER

you can drown without water
you can cry without tears
you've got to dig deeper
and try to overcome your fears

BECOMING HER

becoming the best she
is simple as can be
becoming the best her
means letting go of who you were

PREFERRED REMAINS

you can stay who you are
you can grow and can change
your heart and your soul
are all that remains
the person you are
the person you were
the beauty is that you
get to choose which you prefer

YOUR GRIND

you can take just a minute
you can take all of your time
just get yourself together
and get back to your grind

FORGIVE

forgive yourself for who you were
as long as you've learned
you're better off, I'm sure

WORK IN PROGRESS

She's a work in progress
But really, aren't we all?
How many of us get up and run
Before we learn to crawl?

LACKING

Knowing when to cut back
and knowing when to keep going
are two qualities I lack and
I lack them without knowing

CLEVER

Losing oneself doesn't have to be forever
Just come up with new ways to improve
Get moving, use your brain, be clever

Winter

SNOWMAN

The snowman you built
With your own two hands
Has never been anywhere else
Than where he stands

BLACK HOLE

Where is the snow?
without it, not whole
Where is the snow?
without it, black hole

SNOW

There's a calm in the snow
There's a peace that it brings
There's something inside my brain
That when it sees snow, it sings

A plethora of Randomness

BLOODLESS WOUNDS

Are there wounds that don't bleed?
Of course there are
There are battle wounds you'd never expect
Because they didn't leave the slightest scar

CLOSURE

And just like that
She had all the closure she needed
Just like turning off the TV screen
Except, no fuzzies
Just straight to black
All the closure she never saw coming
now, over her shoulder and behind her back

MEMORIES

Someday, these days will be a memory
Someday, they'll be done and through
Someday, a wish for more time
Will be a constant wish for you

MEMORY GHOST

The toughest hours
The darkest days
They challenged us
in many ways
Through hurt and tears
both, pain and fears
brought us here today
with hope and prayers
multiple layers
to discover truth and love
some may question it but
no doubt there was help from above
family is what matters
family means the most
This can be all behind us
Forever, a memory
Like a ghost

TIME MAY SHAKE

In the end
you may be surprised
who shows up
who's by your side
in the end
fate may twist
time may shake
in the end
you choose who you take

FALLING SOUL

When the darkness is calling
and you can feel it
your soul is falling
it is in, you must reel it
don't let it consume you
this very thing
you're meant to go through

OUT OF TOUCH

Out of touch with being in touch
Can't handle it
Can't fix it
It's simply too much

EASY TO FORGET

Turn the page without concern
Turn without regret
Exhale, remember
it's easy to forget

HER SOUL LET GO

her soul let go of the toxicity
to survive
to breathe
to better herself
her soul let go

MORNING PLEAS

the wind passed through like a calm morning breeze
leaving her to sit with her feelings
and hear the distant, early pleas
for the answer, she knows, is within her heart
but she hates and hates that she has to restart

SO MUCH TO SAY

when there is so much you want to say
but your brain cannot form the words
and you're unable to explain
the hurt
the feelings
the pain

TEST OF STRENGTH

sometimes, you're strong
until you can't be strong anymore
sometimes, your knees give out
and you just hit the floor
when you're down
that's when your mind works best
and you figure out who stands to pass the test
real or fake
love or hate
there forever
or just too late

MEMORY LABEL

when time is lost
and you can't get it back
just one word or visit
can just throw you off track
many memories, now flooding in
feeling emotions, you had buried within
what happens when we're done here
and our time is up
do you see a half empty
of a half full cup
do we go to heaven
do we go to hell
when we get where we're going
all the stories, we can tell
memories will replay
fold out like a screen
life finally has substance
and we know what it means
so cherish these moments
while you're still able
for, one of these days, "memory" will be the label

READ TO ME

when I'm old and can no longer do much for myself
my only request is that my children read to me
even if the doctors say I cannot hear you
I can
I will
keep reading to me
please don't stop reading to me
and when the day of departure comes
when my physical body has to be put in the ground
bury me with those books you read
so I'll always have you around
my spirit may stay
it may even go
but please just keep reading
it's the best way to grow

MEANT TO BE

whether the sun is rising
or the sun is setting
you're the person you're called to be
from the bottom of your heart
to the depths of your soul
allow yourself to be who you need

YOU'VE HANDLED MORE

there are days that seem they will never end
and days when we feel that we'll snap if we bend
but there is always a reason
always a cure
forever, a benefit
to all you endure
the sun, continues to rise
you see nothing but love in your little ones eyes
so go ahead and cry on the bathroom floor
you can handle this
you've handled more

FULL PLATE

you've got so much on your plate
those who can't relate
just hate
their feelings, impossible to navigate
throw stones
call names
I'm officially done with the games
I've said it before
I'll say it again
but just remember
this is because of your mouth, you ran
spewing feelings you harbored inside
just know I never did and I never lied
that's okay
and that's just fine
this is the last
and that was your time
not until she has been cleansed

YOU SLEPT

Nothing is worse than being tired
Wanting to sleep
But it's as if your brain is wired
Random thoughts and reminiscing
Wondering ...
if that one old friend says you're the one they're missing
Why do we only think about these
Things when our eyes just won't seem to close
Because this is insomnia and this is how it goes
Think happy thoughts, count the sheep
But you're just so tired
You could simply weep
You take a breath, relax your head
Turn the thoughts down, get comfy in bed
Before you know it, it's morning
You slept

FROM BOTH ENDS

She's burning the candle from both of its ends
Neglecting her family, her thoughts and her friends
But what else should she be doing with herself right
now
It's like her and the devil have taken a vow
She prays and she prays, to come to the light
She just wants to do everything how she feels is right
But just one more candle, that's all she can burn
Because after that candle, she has nowhere to turn
Don't burn from both ends, something tells her
Take time for yourself, remember who you were
You haven't been lost, you can make a return
But from both ends of the candle, you must not burn.

Words Within the Darkness

DARK

So many tell me that my writings are dark
So many say that, very well I can hide
My emotions, my feelings, the horrible past
I wish I knew when it happened
Those things would not last
So yes, maybe it's true
My writings are dark
And yes, maybe it's true that very well, I hide
What if I said that is false
Would you know that I lied?

BLACK UNICORN

She doesn't write about unicorns and rainbows
For when she sits to write
That's not where her mind goes
It goes to the hurt
The pain and the fears
The trauma that's been done
Will outlast her years

URGE

sometimes, I get the urge
to sit here and write
sometimes, it's real early
and sometimes, at night
but one that I make sure every time
is that every other line
seems to flow or rhyme
the goal of a write
the dream of a poet
making sure it's all perfect
before I post and show it

OOZING WORDS

I don't have to write poetry
it just oozes from my soul
so much in my body
that has to be told

LATE NIGHT WORDS

it's always late night
when the words come to me
they come out so freely and effortlessly
trying my best to put emotions into text
feelings are so hard to feel
when you don't know what's coming next

TEMPORARY STALL

it's not writers block
it's a temporary stall
rising up so high
only to crash into a wall
from a light at the end
to a cold, dark space
only time will tell
continue with grace

DARK AND REAL

So my work is dark
I can't help it, it's how I feel
Yes, my work is dark
Absorb that this is real

DUALITY

I can write you a poem
I can read you a story
I can play either role
The judge or the jury

EXPLANATION

I write to express
I write to feel
The rhythm
The words
they help me to heal
from the things that have hurt me
have burned deep inside
the pain that I've felt
the tears that I've cried
so when I'm questioned on why
I write as much as I do
because it's my therapy
is my explanation to you

ABOUT THE AUTHOR

A.M. Forney is a writer and poet who resides in Pennsylvania with her husband and their three children. When she's not writing, she enjoys music, books and working out.

Follow her on social media at:

Facebook – A.M. FORNEY
Instagram – poetic_bookworm_

The hashtag, #amforney, on Instagram features all of her work.

ACKNOWLEDGMENTS

First and foremost, thank you to 300 South for taking a chance on me with my collection. It means the world.

This project was something I had always dreamed of having published but needed the extra push to do so.

Being a full time, working mother of three, time is fairly limited but thanks to my husband, Brian and best friend, Darby, I was given the added motivation to finally get my poetry out there.

So many people have supported my work over the years but to finally see it come to fruition is beyond amazing. I do not plan for this to be my sole project but being my first officially published one makes it so very special to me. Although there are pieces in this book that hurt to write, I am thankful for all of my life experiences. Every one of them are what made me who I am today.

With that being said, thank you for taking the time to read my poetry.

A. M. Forney